GUNPOWDER JOE

Anthony Clarvoe

BROADWAY PLAY PUBLISHING INC
New York
www.broadwayplaypublishing.com
info@broadwayplaypublishing.com

GUNPOWDER JOE

Cover photo by Bob Rush

First edition: May 2017
Second editon: June 2017
I S B N: 978-0-88145-716-2

Book design: Marie Donovan
Page make-up: Adobe InDesign
Typeface: Palatino
Printed and bound in the U S A

GUNPOWDER JOE was commissioned by Bloomsburg Theatre Ensemble. The world premiere was presented by Bloomsburg Theatre Ensemble (Jon White-Spunner, Managing Director) at the Alvina Krause Theatre, Bloomsburg, PA, on 21 January 2017. The cast and creative contributors were:

JOSEPH PRIESTLEY .... James Goode
MARY PRIESTLEY/TIMOTHY PICKERING
Elizabeth Dowd
THOMAS COOPER .... Eric Wunsch
BENJAMIN FRANKLIN BACHE .... Richard Cannaday
JOHN ADAMS .... Andrew Hubatsek
ABIGAIL ADAMS/WILLIAM COBBETT .... Jubilith Moore
THOMAS JEFFERSON/JUSTICE OF THE PEACE
Daniel Roth
SALLY HEMINGS/MADISON
Amber Reauchean Williams
CHILD .... Irene Combs-Cannaday, Luke Saraçoğlu

Director .... Laurie McCants
Set .... F Elaine Williams
Lights .... Heath Hansum
Costumes .... Paula D Davis
Music & sound .... Steven Gilliland
Choreography .... Kelly Knox
Projections .... Lena Miskulin, Laurie McCants,
J Victoria Nation
Properties .... Melissa Matthews, Emily James,
Eli Raeker-Jordan
Stage Manager .... Jerry Matheny

ACKNOWLEDGMENTS

This project was Laurie McCants's idea, many years ago. It has just kept getting more relevant.

The script includes the words of Joseph Priestley, Abigail Adams, John Adams, Benjamin Franklin Bache, William Cobbett, Thomas Cooper, Thomas Jefferson, and Timothy Pickering. The words of Mary Priestley and Sally Hemings have been lost or suppressed; for them I owe thanks to many sources for reconstruction and advised imagination.

In addition, the script would never have found its present form without four books: *The Invention of Air* by Steven Johnson, *Revolutionary in Exile: The Emigration of Joseph Priestley to America* by Jenny Graham, *The Hemingses of Monticello* by Annette Gordon-Reid, and *American Aurora* by Richard N Rosenfeld.

Bucknell University provided important funding, the whole design team, and Dee Casteel, who tried to help me get the chemistry right. Penn State and Dan Carter offered travel support and, through their Special Collections, the chance to hold Joseph Priestley's manuscripts in my hands. The Friends of Joseph Priestley House and Tom Bresenhan were generous and knowledgeable partners. The Unitarian Universalist Congregation of the Susquehanna Valley and Anne Keeler Evans were inspiring.

The places, Adams National Historical Park, the Chemical Heritage Foundation, the American Philosophical Society, Benjamin Franklin Museum, Joseph Priestley House, and Monticello, taught us things beyond the books.

The Pennsylvania Council for the Arts, which receives important funding from the National Endowment for the Arts, enables this kind of work to be created and seen and taught. Keep fighting for them.

The project owes much to Cassandra Pisieczko.

Nothing is possible without Kate, Sam, and Lucas.

This play is for Bloomsburg Theatre Ensemble and the citizens of Bloomsburg, Pennsylvania.

It is dedicated to Laurie McCants.

CHARACTERS & SETTING

To be played by eight actors

The Priestleys
JOSEPH PRIESTLEY
MARY PRIESTLEY
THOMAS COOPER
MADISON

Massachusetts
JOHN ADAMS
ABIGAIL ADAMS
TIMOTHY PICKERING

Virginia
THOMAS JEFFERSON
SALLY HEMINGS

The Press, etc.
JUSTICE OF THE PEACE
WILLIAM COBBETT
BENJAMIN FRANKLIN BACHE *(pronounced "Beech")*

THOMAS JEFFERSON *doubles* JUSTICE OF THE PEACE; MARY PRIESTLEY *doubles* TIMOTHY PICKERING; ABIGAIL ADAMS *doubles* WILLIAM COBBETT; SALLY HEMINGS *doubles* MADISON. ENSEMBLE *also play* SERVANTS, CITIZENS, *etc., as noted.*

Time & place: Birmingham, England, 1791
United States of America, 1794-1801

NOTES

On design: Fluidity and lightness. Sometimes the action occurs in several places at once and a character who refers to one, while being in another, may travel between them.

Characters are doubled, sometimes with women playing male characters.

Paper is vital: newspapers, broadsides, scientific papers, pamphlets, letters, sermons.

On historical drama: The public actions depicted are matters of historical record. But one thing we know for certain is that what these people said and did in public is not all they said and did. We can infer some of the things they must have done in private, though they didn't speak of them in public. Where they are silent, or have been silenced, it is up to us to imagine the things they might have said and done, in order to do the things we know they did. While we try not to contradict the historical record, we are not obliged to confine ourselves to it.

On drama versus biography: historiography and documentary are expected to limit themselves to presenting an accurate version—by which is usually meant, a defensible interpretation—of historical figures. In historical drama, on the other hand, those real-life figures serve as the basis for created characters whose actions can coincide only partially with those of their namesakes. A dramatic character is both more and less than a person; a character is not merely who a person was; it is also in some way what we take them to represent. One must stand for many. Their actions are not literal, but figurative.

Given all that, this is what happened.

Dreams have their seat in some region of the brain more deeply seated than that which is occupied by our waking thoughts.
Joseph Priestley

ACT ONE

PROLOGUE: THE RIOT

(Sounds of shouts and breakage. Ragged distant singing of God Save the King, *coming and going and getting gradually louder through the scene.)*

(The PRIESTLEYS' *house in Birmingham)*

*(*JOSEPH *and* MARY PRIESTLEY, THOMAS COOPER, *and several* SERVANTS. *All but* JOSEPH *are watching at windows or quickly gathering whatever they can.* COOPER *has been running.)*

COOPER: They are coming this way.

MARY: Can you see?

COOPER: I see flames from the next house. They are less than a mile now.

MARY: We can take the carriage. There is still time.

JOSEPH: Will they damage the house?

*(*JOSEPH PRIESTLEY *speaks with a working class Yorkshire accent. When he is anxious, he stammers a bit. He is not stammering now.)*

MARY: The most important thing is to get you away.

JOSEPH: It will be fine. They have been content to hang me in effigy for years.

MARY: They may be done pretending.

COOPER: Half the dissenters' homes in Birmingham are on fire. Our meeting house is a ruin.

JOSEPH: I cannot be convinced that they will truly harm me.

MARY: We need to make an educated guess here.

COOPER: We need to go!

JOSEPH: Mister Cooper, you've been out there. Do we know who they are?

COOPER: Townsmen, craftsmen, farmers.

JOSEPH: Those are our people, working people.

MARY: I don't think those are religious dissenters out there.

COOPER: They are shouting Church and King.

JOSEPH: So not our people.

COOPER: That is the great English nation out there, calling for our heads.

MARY: How much of the apparatus have we gotten out?

COOPER: We scouted the road. They turned us back.

MARY: Get as much into the cellars as you can.

*(*COOPER *runs out.* MARY *rifles quickly through papers and stuffs most of them into the fireplace.)*

JOSEPH: What are you doing?

MARY: Burning my letters. You should be doing the same.

(A particularly loud sound of breakage and cheering.)

MARY: Listen to that. The hatred.

JOSEPH: It is not personal. They need someone to blame for how the world is changing and the church and the government tell them to blame me. But why now?

MARY: The newspapers.

JOSEPH: Many a fire is started with newspapers.

(A fist pounds on a door. Terrified silence)

VOICE: *(Off)* Justice of the Peace! Open up!

MARY: Thank God.

(JUSTICE OF THE PEACE *enters, trailed by* COOPER.*)*

JUSTICE: Church and King.

COOPER & MARY: *(Reluctantly)* Church and King.

MARY: Thank you for coming.

JOSEPH: Yes, thank God.

JUSTICE: Just what I need, a Unitarian blessing.

MARY: We are glad the authorities have sent someone official.

JUSTICE: Officially I am not even here.

MARY: But you have come to help us?

JUSTICE: Doctor Joseph Priestley. I am here to inform you that you are disturbing the peace.

JOSEPH: We are sitting quietly in our home.

JUSTICE: Your presence is causing violence and looting.

MARY: It is our fault we are being attacked?

JUSTICE: I am here to prevent a bloodbath. I want no French style justice in my jurisdiction. Time to go.

MARY: Sir, there is a fortune in scientific apparatus in this house. A fortune in books. Decades of research and writing. This laboratory has earned millions of pounds for English industry, thousands of jobs. None of it is worth a shilling without the mind of this man here.

COOPER: These people don't know what they are doing.

MARY: This region has grown rich off his ideas.

JUSTICE: The people outside have not grown rich.

COOPER: We are running out of time.

MARY: We have a carriage. We can ride to the inn and wait there for the coach to London.

(A SERVANT *runs out.)*

JUSTICE: Not the inn. I would not recommend letting yourselves be seen in town today.

JOSEPH: Where can we go? I would not put any of our friends at risk by sheltering me.

COOPER: Many of them have fled already.

MARY: Can we get to London? The congregation there will hide us.

JOSEPH: Hiding suggests I am a fugitive from justice.

JUSTICE: My men are outnumbered. And they are unwilling to risk their lives in defense of a man who has called for the overthrow of their church and their king.

JOSEPH: But I didn't. I only ask if these institutions are necessary.

JUSTICE: They are going to burn this house. You asked if the king is necessary? You're about to get your answer. Listen to them. They are drunk and mad with rage.

JOSEPH: They are so frightened. Those poor people.

JUSTICE: Run. Disappear.

(Everyone moves to go. JOSEPH *stands where he is.)*

JOSEPH: I do not fear for my own safety.

MARY: Oh, for—

JUSTICE: You'd better.

JOSEPH: But any harm these people do will harm their souls as well. You must help to stop them, for their own good. God has given them into our keeping, sir.

*(*JUSTICE *and* JOSEPH *look at each other. Absolute conviction on both sides. The sounds of riot are very loud now.)*

JUSTICE: Damn it! Is he always like this?

MARY: Every day.

JUSTICE: I will hold them at the door as long as I can. Run.

JOSEPH: Bless you, sir.

JUSTICE: Go to hell. *(Striding out, shouting)* Church and King! Church and King!

COOPER: We will stay if you want, Doctor, and try to defend the house.

MARY: Dearest, if you stay, Mister Cooper will stay, the boys will stay. Our boys will die defending you.

JOSEPH: Can't have that.

COOPER: But the books, the apparatus.

JOSEPH: No, no. Merely things. While I have you all I want for nothing. It will be fine.

MARY: Let's go.

JOSEPH: Oh my poor country.

FIZZ

*(*JOSEPH *and* MARY *are joined by the* ENSEMBLE, *now as American dignitaries. Among them are* JOHN *and* ABIGAIL ADAMS, THOMAS JEFFERSON, *and* BENJAMIN FRANKLIN BACHE *[pronounced "Beech"].)*

*(*BENNY BACHE *wears bifocals, no wig, and rumpled clothing. He is young, but cultivates a look strikingly*

reminiscent of Benjamin Franklin. He holds his newspaper, the Aurora, and speaks to us.)

BACHE: The name of Joseph Priestley will be long remembered among all enlightened people. England will regret her ungrateful treatment to this venerable and illustrious man.

JOHN: Welcome, Doctor Priestley, Mrs Priestley.

BACHE: His persecutions in England have brought him to the American Republic as a safe and honorable retreat in his declining years.

THOMAS: On behalf of the Commonwealth of Virginia.

JOHN: The Commonwealth of Massachusetts.

BACHE: The City of Philadelphia, the most beautiful city in America, that gave the world my grandfather. Benjamin Franklin Bache, at your service, Doctor.

JOSEPH: Benjamin Franklin! He was one of the dearest men in the world to me.

BACHE: He felt the same of you. "Doctor Priestley, my favorite heretic." I inherited his printing business. Publisher and editor and head writer of the *Philadelphia Aurora.*

JOHN: Doctor Priestley, we have met, if you cast your mind back many years. John Adams.

JOSEPH: Bless my soul, Mister Adams.

ABIGAIL: Vice President Adams.

JOSEPH: Vice President Adams. You were the American ambassador in London, so long ago now.

JOHN: We have grown old, Doctor.

JOSEPH: But soon your country will be…what do you call it? Electing a new President. Aye? This is the most extraordinary experiment.

MARY: Speaking of experiments? All is in readiness.

(An apparatus of a vat, bottles, and tubes. MARY *assists and prompts as* JOSEPH *demonstrates.)*

JOSEPH: Now, I do not have a practical head. As a religious dissenter, I was not allowed to have regular schooling. So I had to learn to reckon for myself. I have some friends who contribute to my maintenance, and I do some thinking for them. They make those thoughts into money. Electrical power, I thought about that for a while.

MARY: With your friend Doctor Franklin.

JOSEPH: When I was but a young bumpkin in London, Benjamin Franklin was my inspiration.

MARY: Franklin, the kite, and the key in the thunderstorm. Who wrote that story and gave it to the world?

JOSEPH: I did.

MARY: Appointed to the Royal Society. Won the Copley Medal.

JOSEPH: Contributions to scientific knowledge.

MARY: And inventions of much practical use! Such as…

JOSEPH: Aye. From the beginning of time, mankind believed that water was water, and earth was earth, and air was air. But look: *(Demonstrating with his apparatus)* We take this vessel, completely full of ordinary water. *(Showing phial)* From the Earth, we take this chalk. We add water to it, and a little oil of vitriol, and from this earth we free a kind of air, that has been part of it, trapped in it. *(Manipulating pipes and bottles)* Now, if we lead this air, freed from the earth, through this pipe, into the vessel of ordinary water, *(Shaking the vessel vigorously)* and we agitate it vigorously—this is very important—we must agitate. Agitate. This new, freed air now combines with the water, and gives it a kind of…liveliness.

*(*MARY *hands around glasses of seltzer.)*

MARY: Which aids the digestion like water from the finest spa resorts.

JOSEPH: Carbonated beverages. It might go somewhere.

(Applause and a belch or two from the ENSEMBLE.*)*

JOSEPH: Things we thought unchangeable are made of many elements. Invisible to the eye. Under the pressure of experiment, they reveal themselves as they truly are. Just as you are here. Just as they are in France.

BACHE: What is your position on the revolution in France?

JOSEPH: In France they are conducting a great experiment in human freedom.

MARY: But we were speaking of experiments with air. Your greatest discovery…

JOSEPH: Aye. Dephlogisticated air, I discovered that, though it's become better known by a different name that I will never accept. Oxygen. So named by the other great discoverer of air. Lavoisier. A Frenchman. I gave him the idea. A brilliant man. He is likely to make many great discoveries of his own, once he acknowledges his error about phlogiston.

BACHE: Doctor Priestley. Have you not heard?

JOHN: We just got word ourselves. It must have happened when you were at sea.

BACHE: Lavoisier is dead.

JOSEPH: Lavoisier. How? A laboratory accident?

BACHE: They cut off his head.

JOSEPH: The new government?

ABIGAIL: The new revolutionary government.

JOSEPH: Why?

JOHN: He was an aristocrat.

ABIGAIL: All part of the great experiment in freedom.

JOSEPH: Oh dear. Oh dear.

BACHE: You chose the right place to move, Doctor Priestley.

JOSEPH: Yes. Your country and England, at last, are no longer at war.

JOHN: We have a treaty with England. The merchants are happy. They can trade with England.

THOMAS: But not everyone is happy. Especially our old ally France.

JOSEPH: France and England, forever at war.

MARY: We are eager to settle here.

JOHN: Consider Boston, Doctor! The Athens of America!

BACHE: Philadelphia, our nation's capital!

THOMAS: Virginia.

JOSEPH: Now, Virginia, aye. Virginia is, I believe you call it a… "slave state?"

(MARY coughs.)

JOSEPH: Bless you, dearest. *(To* THOMAS*)* Do I have that right?

ABIGAIL: Does he have that right, Mister Jefferson?

THOMAS: Slavery, it grieves me to say, remains legal all over this country.

ABIGAIL: Not in Massachusetts.

JOSEPH: Splendid, I have written and thought about slavery for many years, but I have never met a, what do you call yourself, a "slaver"? And I know opinions here are sharply divided. Aye? What is your position on slavery, Mrs Adams?

ABIGAIL: My parents owned slaves. We freed them. Some things are simply wrong.

THOMAS: Wrong, yes. But not simply wrong.

JOSEPH: Sir?

THOMAS: One inherits debts and obligations.

JOHN: Our friend Mister Jefferson keeps slaves.

ABIGAIL: Or rather they keep him. His life of philosophy depends on them to keep it up. *(She departs, nodding to* THOMAS, *not without affection.)*

THOMAS: What we have discovered in America, Doctor: there is no land that is not already peopled. The people and the place are inextricable.

JOSEPH: Nothing we can see is a single thing.

MARY: We have a place all chosen. Our friend Thomas Cooper and our sons have a tract of land in a thriving community on the Susquehanna River. An easy journey from Philadelphia.

JOSEPH: Where we hope soon to welcome you all.

(ENSEMBLE *toasts with soda water.)*

ENSEMBLE MEMBERS: Doctor Joseph Priestley!

PORCUPINE

*(*WILLIAM COBBETT. *Working class, ex-British Army. He brandishes a newspaper and addresses us.)*

COBBETT: Doctor Joseph Priestley, the Firebrand Philosopher, is new arrived from England. Those who have not read his philosophy or heard his sermons may wonder what he says. Well, try this and I quote: "We are laying gunpowder, grain by grain, under the old building of error and superstition, which a single spark may one day inflame; that building, the work of ages, may be overturned in a moment." That old building he's talking about? That's the Church of England. Christianity. That old ruin. Joseph Priestley. Gunpowder Joe.

(TIMOTHY PICKERING *joins* COBBETT.)

(COBBETT *is reckless and ruthless and a bad man to have as an enemy.* PICKERING *is incomparably more dangerous.)*

PICKERING: Strong stuff.

COBBETT: I've got nothing against the foreigners as such.

PICKERING: You're a foreigner, Mister Cobbett.

COBBETT: I'm English born, proud to say it. Editor, publisher, and head writer of the most entertaining political broadsheet in these United States: *Peter Porcupine's Gazette*. Peter Porcupine, my quill is my weapon. You the police?

PICKERING: Not exactly.

COBBETT: You look like somebody who works for somebody.

PICKERING: Some people, people whose names might surprise you, enjoy what you write about the foreigners. They believe you are working for the betterment of the United States. Doctor Priestley…

COBBETT: Gunpowder Joe.

PICKERING: Yes, good, has attacked the laws of England in print.

COBBETT: And declared his sentiments in favor of those butchers in France. Thousands die, weltering in blood, and the philosopher cheers the show.

PICKERING: And now he walks among us, safe and free. What will he do next?

COBBETT: I would do anything. To make sure what happened to France never happens here.

PICKERING: Keep doing what you're doing. There's money.

COBBETT: Not so much.

PICKERING: There will be now.

NORTHUMBERLAND

*(*JOSEPH *and* COOPER *look over things.)*

JOSEPH: Mister Cooper. You did tell us Northumberland was a thriving community.

COOPER: It is. By American standards. Basic necessities, enormous potential for growth.

JOSEPH: No meeting halls, no coffee houses, no bookstalls, none of the places people meet to explore the questions of the day.

COOPER: There are two chapels, Quaker and Wesleyan. A grocery, a brewery, a clockmaker, a potter. A potash manufacturer.

JOSEPH: We will at least have few distractions.

*(*MARY *enters.)*

MARY: Mister Cooper, you told us Northumberland was an easy journey from Philadelphia.

COOPER: Yes, again, "easy" in the American sense.

MARY: We will have few interruptions.

COOPER: You wanted a safe place.

MARY: We are giving up a great deal for safety.

JOSEPH: As any refugee must. We can go back to holding church services in our home, love.

MARY: As we did when we began.

COOPER: We are in America now. I mean to be an American. We can sit and complain or we can set to work improving the place. There is a printing press.

MARY: Have you given any more thought to starting a school?

JOSEPH: I have written to my patrons in England, asking for funding.

MARY: I am sure my brother will help.

JOSEPH: But in the meantime, what are we to do?

COOPER: I am trying to get permission to do my work, as a lawyer. Thus far, nothing. I do not know why. I know a man with a printing press, close by.

MARY: Concentrate your energies on science. Rather than politics or religion, just for a while?

JOSEPH: True. If I am going to correct the persistent errors about phlogiston.

MARY: Yes, good. Work on that.

JOSEPH: I must replace at least some of the laboratory apparatus and my library.

MARY: Well then.

(MARY takes a scrap of paper and pencil and begins to sketch designs for a house.)

COOPER: People need to hear you. They think they know you and they don't know half.

MARY: The half they know is more than enough. We are guests here.

JOSEPH: Believe me, love. I pray that for once in our lives we may live in peace.

MARY: That was the point of this settlement, wasn't it? I love it, the quiet. I do hope more families will join ours.

COOPER: I want to live someplace just.

JOSEPH: We shall all live someplace perfectly just, forever.

MARY: If we behave ourselves.

COOPER: But to ask a mind like his and a spirit like mine to "behave ourselves." It is much to ask.

MARY: You have a family, Mister Cooper, it is they who are asking. And you, dearest, already they are writing against you, this Peter Porcupine person –

JOSEPH: He is writing things about me that are untrue. I must correct him.

MARY: He writes that you are political. You write, debating his points. So now you are being political, and you have proved his point!

COOPER: This country is at war with itself. Mister Adams and his friends want a stronger Federal government, more manufactures, more trade, and so more international presence, a navy. Mister Jefferson and his friends want stronger state governments, more agriculture. We have a duty to speak our minds.

MARY: And what if no one wants to hear? I will design us a home and have it built. It will not be England, but it will do. Our sons are out there, trying to learn to farm. I am frightened for them. Will you two promise me to try to keep the peace?

COOPER: If I promise to publish nothing under my own name.

MARY: And nothing that announces where you are. If it comes from Northumberland, everyone will know it is you or you. I do not want this place to become a notorious nest of rebels.

JOSEPH: I agree.

COOPER: And I.

MARY: Thank you. Now let us find some work that we can do.

THE POWER OF THE PRESS

*(*COBBETT *and* BACHE *both hold their own newspapers:* BACHE *the Aurora,* COBBETT *Porcupine's Gazette.)*

COBBETT: From *Porcupine's Gazette*: The charge that Doctor Priestley brought against England is, that it did not offer him protection from the mob. Would he prefer a revolutionary tribunal in France? Villains that sit in mock judgment, their sleeves tucked up to their elbows, even the goblets they drink from besmeared with human blood!

BACHE: From the *Aurora*: Why does Peter Porcupine publish what he knows to be fake?

COBBETT: Benjamin Franklin Bache. Lightning Rod Junior. I feel nothing but contempt—

BACHE: This liar and scoundrel—

COBBETT: The world knows Bache is a liar; a fallen wretch; and therefore we should always treat him as we would a Turk, a Jew, a Frenchman or a Dog.

BACHE: Or a Porcupine! Who would believe the news he hears from a burrowing forest animal?

COBBETT: Bache has outraged every principle of decency, morality, religion, and nature. The boys should spit on him as he goes along the street, but that would do him too much honor. *(He exits.)*

BACHE: And that, ladies and gentlemen, is the most popular journalist in America. Why? Why do people only want to read news that they already know? Lies they already believe? And how am I supposed to compete with that? I don't mind taking sides, but when the other side is such a long way to the side, how far do you have to go? I guess we'll find out.

THREE HOUSEHOLDS

(Simultaneously:)

(Northumberland: JOSEPH *examines a mineral sample.* MARY *is on the move. A chess board is set up, mid-game.)*

(Quincy: JOHN *goes through newspapers,* ABIGAIL *letters.)*

(Monticello: THOMAS *and* SALLY *read and mend, respectively.)*

BACHE: Besides. My grandfather told me America is a set of experiments. *(He passes through each place.)*

(First, Northumberland)

JOSEPH: The new mineral samples have come.

MARY: Then your laboratory will need to be made ready.

JOSEPH: Stay. Rest.

MARY: Soon.

JOSEPH: Your cough has come back.

*(*MARY *moves a chess piece.)*

MARY: Check.

*(*JOSEPH *hands* BACHE *a pamphlet.)*

JOSEPH: If you care to, my latest. *(To* MARY*)* I see what you're up to.

MARY: Do you, dearest?

*(*JOSEPH *stares at the chessboard.* MARY *exits.)*

*(*BACHE *crosses to Quincy. He is not there, except in spirit.)*

BACHE: As Grandfather said: a set of experiments.

ABIGAIL: The new dispatches have come. If France does not cease these attacks on our shipping…

JOHN: Washington will not declare war.

ABIGAIL: Of course not. We may need to.

JOHN: When I am president, I will send envoys to negotiate an end to these attacks.

ABIGAIL: In the meantime…

JOHN: We are not ready for war.

ABIGAIL: So. Preparations.

JOHN: Build a standing army? A navy?

ABIGAIL: Warships. "Our wooden walls." You are a good New England man. Power rides the sea.

JOHN: That will take a lot of money. The people will be angry.

ABIGAIL: But our friends will earn a lot of money. Our people will be happy.

JOHN: *(Reading a newspaper)* Listen to this. "Vice President Adams is old, bald,—

*(*BACHE *joins in, reciting from memory.)*

JOHN & BACHE: …blind, toothless, and crippled!"

ABIGAIL: If that fellow and his newspaper are not suppressed, we shall come to a civil war!

JOHN: A free press maintains the majesty of the people.

ABIGAIL: That is not journalism. That is terrorism. Well. You are the sweetest man. No one knows but me.

JOHN: No one.

ABIGAIL: I do not make you contented.

JOHN: If anything did, you would. Nothing does.

ABIGAIL: Perhaps if you had married a rich wife, like Washington.

JOHN: Washington. Explain Washington.

ABIGAIL: No one can.

JOHN: You get silly around him.

ABIGAIL: Everyone does.

JOHN: What does everyone see in him? We had more dashing soldiers, more brilliant commanders. He can barely speak. Explain him.

ABIGAIL: He is very tall.

JOHN: Is that it?

ABIGAIL: At our country's birth, we needed a great man, and he looks like one.

JOHN: I know we've had this conversation many times.

ABIGAIL: In every crisis, these shallow men have had the sense to turn to you. You have been every great man's trusted second. Now it is your turn. They are about to elect you to be their President.

JOHN: The second president. Story of my life.

ABIGAIL: Every great man, in the end, is remembered for one deed, one bold stroke. Electricity, the Declaration, Crossing the Delaware. You are a great man. Your great deed simply must lie in the future. You will do such things.

(JOHN *broods.* ABIGAIL *suffers with him.)*

(BACHE *crosses to Monticello, speaking to* THOMAS.)

(SALLY *watches.)*

(BACHE *passes the pamphlet to* THOMAS *who opens it.)*

BACHE: Priestley publishes, but mostly science, and not much of consequence. He keeps trying to convince people phlogiston exists. A substance in everything flammable, the element of burning. He keeps trying to poke holes in oxygen. All these old revolutionaries, clinging to what they know.

THOMAS: Keep the heat under Mister Adams. And publish what you can supporting Priestley.

BACHE: It will make him more of a target.

THOMAS: *(Reading, not listening)* Now this is interesting.

(As he goes, BACHE *turns to take in the scene:* THOMAS *and* SALLY. *To us:)*

BACHE: Of course, the most dangerous experiments are carried out in secret. *(He exits.)*

SALLY: I should tell you. I'm carrying again.

THOMAS: Are you well?

SALLY: This one feels stronger than the others. I'm carrying high, so it may be a boy this time.

THOMAS: Congratulations.

SALLY: You made me a promise. In France.

THOMAS: I remember.

SALLY: I didn't have to come back here. I could have stayed there. Been free. A French woman.

THOMAS: Many of them have lost their heads. You gambled right, coming back here.

SALLY: Did I?

THOMAS: Your children will be free. Upon my death.

SALLY: No, not upon your death. That was not what we said.

THOMAS: And why not?

SALLY: You owe people money. A lot of money.

THOMAS: How do you know that?

SALLY: Everybody knows that. If your family sells my children to pay your debts…

THOMAS: That will not happen.

SALLY: Don't wait till you die. Free your children. Are we agreed?

THOMAS: I am sure we are.

ELECTRICITY

(JOSEPH stands near an imposing and beautiful static electricity generator. MARY is nearby, visibly wearier.)

JOSEPH: Ladies and gentlemen, I am grateful for the chance to present to you the plans for our proposed Northumberland Academy. My reputation as a minister, a scientist, and a political phil—

(MARY coughs.)

JOSEPH: —as a philosopher has spread to these shores. Yet, my first and most important employment was as a teacher. To open a school to serve the youth of Pennsylvania would enable me to feel that I am serving well the country that has offered me safe haven.

MARY: We need your help and support to make this school a reality.

JOSEPH: Aye. And. While you weigh your decision, allow me to present a sample of the manner of scientific knowledge this academy will offer the youth of your nation. As some of you know, my original apparatus was destroyed or left behind in England.

MARY: But here, painstakingly reconstructed—

JOSEPH: And in some ways improved, is my device for generating that modern miracle, that lightning in a bottle, that bolt from the blue, electricity.

(JOSEPH and MARY demonstrate the powers of static electricity.)

JOSEPH: If you want the youth of this state and this nation to learn how to wield this power we are taking from the heavens, please consider a generous donation toward the creation of the Northumberland Academy. We thank you for your attention.

(MARY *stifles a cough and exits hurriedly.)*

(JOSEPH *watches her go.)*

THE SERVANT PROBLEM

*(*COOPER *enters, reading printed pages.)*

COOPER: Could there be tea? I'm parched.

JOSEPH: I don't know.

COOPER: The new *Porcupine's Gazette* has come. It seems we are both very dangerous men. What?

JOSEPH: Mary has never been herself since our youngest died.

COOPER: Can't you get her more help?

JOSEPH: No one will work for me.

COOPER: Have you considered a slave?

JOSEPH: I couldn't possibly. I have written in opposition to the slave trade. And Pennsylvania outlawed slavery.

COOPER: There are people in this area who own slaves.

JOSEPH: There are?

COOPER: Openly.

JOSEPH: How can that be?

COOPER: There are loopholes in the law. So the good men of Pennsylvania could be seen to pass the kind of law that good men pass, without actually changing anything affecting themselves. But that is just a hypothesis that I have. So there are slaves.

JOSEPH: We will not buy one.

COOPER: No. We can hire one.

JOSEPH: How can you hire a slave? A slave is unpaid by definition.

COOPER: You rent the slave. Like a room at an inn. For your temporary use. You pay the person who owns the slave. *(Calling)* Madison?

*(*MADISON *enters and stands.)*

COOPER: Madison, this is Doctor Priestley.

JOSEPH: Cooper. This is wrong.

COOPER: Madison, would you go to the kitchen and see if you can put together some tea?

JOSEPH: Thank you?

*(*MADISON *exits.)*

COOPER: There are two wrongs here. One you are doing now: limiting the use you are making of your talents by wasting time doing tasks anyone could do. The other wrong, if it is a wrong, would be done to a stranger.

JOSEPH: He is not a stranger. We have been introduced.

COOPER: Madison. Who is already enslaved. Who has, at the moment, not enough to do. And perhaps a cruel master. Would time spent with us be not actually an improvement in Madison's situation?

JOSEPH: That is possible. But…to benefit from the slave trade.

COOPER: You already benefit from the slave trade. That shirt is made of cotton cloth. The cotton is grown by slaves. We could buy cloth made by farmers who work their own land, but that would cost more than we can pay. So. We hire slaves already. The wrong is already done. This would only mean that you would see it.

JOSEPH: We could try. Maybe some good will come of it.

COOPER: Yes. It would be an experiment. So that's all right then.

JOSEPH: I am troubled. But I do not see any other solution.

COOPER: Good. A slave it is then.

*(*MADISON *enters, with tea things.)*

COOPER: That was quick.

*(*JOSEPH *pours, and brings* COOPER *a cup as he speaks.)*

COOPER: *(To us)* Listen. People think how things occur, the things in newspapers, history. That it's people riding horses, waving swords. People making speeches, passing laws. No. *(Taking the teacup)* Thank you. This, here, is what occurs. The swords and the speeches, that's all just results.

THE BOOK OF JOB

*(*ENSEMBLE *sings a sad song as the stage transforms.)*

*(*MARY *slumps in a chair, very ill.* JOSEPH *sits by* MARY.*)*

JOSEPH: Thou sayest to diseases, Go, and they go; Come, and they come, to answer the wise and gracious purposes of thy providence—

MARY: *(Delirious)* Shh.

JOSEPH: Hello, love.

MARY: Shhh.

JOSEPH: Are you feeling any better? What can I bring you?

MARY: Hush, child. Your father is philosophizing. Mustn't interrupt your Father while he is philosophizing.

JOSEPH: Mary. Do you ever wish we were home?

MARY: We are home. When you've buried a child in a place, that's your place now.

JOSEPH: Our son

JOHN: Our daughters

ABIGAIL: How can we grieve so for a person we barely knew?

SALLY: When you lay your hopes to rest in a place

THOMAS: My wife, my daughter

SALLY: His wife my half-sister, his daughter my niece. And our daughters. Ours.

THOMAS: The people and the place are inextricable.

SALLY: The place where you sat on the floor and wept.

JOHN: That's your place now.

ABIGAIL: Where you got up and had to start living again.

*(*MARY *coughs. She doubles over with the coughing. Waving off* JOSEPH, *she exits. Music trickles out.)*

JOSEPH: My wife
My wife was a woman of an excellent understanding much improved by reading, of great fortitude and strength of mind, and of a temper in the highest degree affectionate and generous. She entirely relieved me of every concern. I was always only a guest in her house.

(All that are left are JOSEPH *and* COOPER.*)*

COOPER: Our plans for this settlement have come to nothing. Our friends have settled elsewhere. The money is not coming.

JOSEPH: No one will sponsor the Northumberland Academy.

COOPER: I am not allowed to practice law. I am a stranger to them here.

JOSEPH: The new president is an old friend of mine. I can ask him to help you.

COOPER: And you?

JOSEPH: My wife died and is buried here. I will never live with her in the house she designed. I will live here until I can join her, when my labors are done.

COOPER: Your apparatus is here. And there is a printing press. We could do great things.

(COBBETT *enters and watches them go.)*

COBBETT: There is something so pathetic, so irresistibly moving in all this that a man must have a hard heart indeed to read of it, and not burst into laughter.
I hope I shall see the malignant old Tartuffe of Northumberland begging his bread through the streets of Philadelphia, and ending his days in the poorhouse, without a friend to close his eyes.

(PICKERING *joins* COBBETT.)

PICKERING: My compliments. Thanks in large part to you, Doctor Priestley is gaining a reputation as the most dangerous radical in America. And now if you are interested in another project…

COBBETT: I'm listening.

PICKERING: I wonder if you would use your powers of description on Thomas Jefferson.

COBBETT: Jefferson. You're worried about Jefferson.

PICKERING: Every freedom-loving American is worried about Thomas Jefferson. He came very close to winning the last election. We mustn't risk his doing better in the next one.

COBBETT: Thomas Jefferson spent too much time in Paris. He's barely an American anymore.

PICKERING: That's the idea.

(PICKERING *exits.)*

COBBETT: Speaking of Paris. The revolutionary government has been doing so much better than the terrible old king. Under the king, people were starving in the streets, rioting for bread.
But now, in the new revolutionary France, people are starving in the streets, rioting for bread. Ready for a revolution against the revolution. So what happens? Troops march into Paris. One young commander orders his men to fire their cannons into the crowd. Blows them to pieces. For being hungry. Can you imagine what happened to that young man? They promoted him. Gave him command of the whole army. General Napoleon Bonaparte.

REVELATION

(JOHN ADAMS *and* JOSEPH PRIESTLEY, *at breakfast.)*

JOSEPH: But what shall I call you now?

JOHN: Not having traditions, we are constantly in surprise, at all the things we don't know how to do.

JOSEPH: You are a head of state.

JOHN: "Your Excellency" has been suggested.

JOSEPH: Your Excellency.

JOHN: Mrs. Adams refers to me as The President. I can be sitting there. "The President's teacup is empty."

JOSEPH: You will be in my prayers.

JOHN: There are days. My vision darkens. Just between us. My Blue Devils.

JOSEPH: Of course.

JOHN: It's a cruel business I'm in.

JOSEPH: It will be fine.

JOHN: That is what Franklin always said.

JOSEPH: He was a supremely confident man. He had reason to be.

JOHN: Yes yes.

JOSEPH: So do you.

JOHN: You are surprisingly kind. I don't know how closely you follow the newspapers.

JOSEPH: They certainly follow after me.

JOHN: Ha. You and me both!

JOSEPH: Why do some men give them so much pleasure in the hunt and others not?

JOHN: In truth, no one escapes. They make you prominent and they make you pay. You know we have a treaty with England. England is at war with France. We have tried to stay neutral. France sees this treaty as an alliance between us and England. The French are attacking our shipping. It may come to war. You are known as a supporter of France.

JOSEPH: Their Revolution, their Republic. Not Terrorism. When I called for revolution, the word meant something different than it does now.

JOHN: If you could only see your way clear to say so in public. It would make a great difference.

JOSEPH: I wish a pulpit were open to me. If I were invited to preach, perhaps you would attend. It would be a great honor.

JOHN: But we were speaking of the news from France.

JOSEPH: Aye. I see in the French Revolution a new era opening in the world. I believe the millennium is near.

JOHN: On what grounds?

JOSEPH: Revelation and the prophecies. The ten horns of the great Beast in the Book of Revelation mean the ten crowned heads of Europe. The execution of the king of France is the falling off of the first of those horns. The nine monarchies of Europe will fall one after another in the same way. The judgments of God are abroad in the earth… As I said: I am not political.

JOHN: No, Doctor. You are not.

JOSEPH: Now, my friend Mister Cooper—

JOHN: Thomas Cooper. We should speak about him. He grows notorious.

JOSEPH: He would make an excellent addition to your administration.

JOHN: You want me to give him a job.

JOSEPH: There is a position in Pennsylvania that requires a legal mind.

JOHN: I would never give such a position to a foreigner.

JOSEPH: He is a naturalized American, I believe.

JOHN: Many able men, Americans—

JOSEPH: None more able than Cooper.

JOHN: Pray do not interrupt me, Doctor. Loyal Americans are seeking these jobs.

(JOSEPH's stammer grows more noticeable.)

JOSEPH: We are loyal. We have given up the country of our birth.

JOHN: You change your loyalty when it suits your convenience! You and your country had a difference of opinion and you abandoned her! Why are you surprised when men suspect you? You claim that Cooper, an alien, will be loyal to me. But where are the proofs? Eh? Where are your proofs? With no evidence, what am I to do? Eh? What am I to do?

SOON TO BE THE MOST FAMOUS ENSLAVED PERSON IN THE WORLD

(SALLY HEMINGS *paces in the near-dark, nursing a baby.)*

SALLY: What to do, what to do. Sleepy boy, one day you will ask yourself. "I'm a man. What am I to do?" Chances are you will be a tall man. They'll want you for fights. And how will you decide? "What would I do, if I were me, and I look like I do with a body like mine? What should such a fine person do with himself?"

So.

Once there was a boy, and that boy is you, and that boy has two uncles. Both of them bought their freedom from your father. Your Uncle Robert, he headed down the hill to Richmond and there he stays, working the same work he worked for your father. Your father can't understand why your Uncle Robert took all the trouble, just to do the same as he'd always done. Well, Uncle Robert has a woman down there, he wanted to marry her, and have children, and just live.

But your Uncle James, now, he wanted to see the world. Baltimore, Philadelphia, New York. No place could hold him. He's in Spain now. Spain.

Or.

When I was just a little girl, your father and his friends had a fight with the King of England. And while they did, some of my uncles and cousins and people, they rose up. Rose up and ran off from my father, and your

father, and George Washington. They joined the King's army and they fought George Washington, fought my father, fought your father. It was a big family fight. And then some of them went to Canada. Some of them had to go home. But some of them went to Africa.
Africa.
Or. There is me.
I have had children. You, yes, you. I have seen the world. London, Paris. And there I saw your father's friends, those Franklins and Adamses. That Mrs. Adams, oh, she did not like me. She was all "What is the use of this girl! She is dashing up and down this house and what has gotten into her?" I had just set my foot in a strange land where no one was slaves and she wanted to know what had gotten into me. I know those people. But they will never know me. You will know me. And I will know you.
A lot of people, if it's their family or their freedom, they will choose their people. You're my people. I choose you.
You, yes, you, think of all those things that you might try.
And you ask yourself: what would I do, if I were me?

FOREIGN RELATIONS

(JOHN *is reading documents.)*

(PICKERING *watches, poised.)*

(ABIGAIL *enters.)*

ABIGAIL: There you are.

(JOHN *holds up a hand.)*

ABIGAIL: What is happening?

PICKERING: The dispatches from Paris have been decoded.

ABIGAIL: And? And? Pickering?

(JOHN *throws down papers and paces the room.)*

PICKERING: It is all a game of chess by mail.

ABIGAIL: Dearest?

JOHN: Never liked those people, never did. Straight dealing? Christian virtues? No no no.

PICKERING: They will not meet our ambassadors—

JOHN: Who are there to negotiate a peace! Peace!

PICKERING: The French foreign minister—

ABIGAIL: Talleyrand.

PICKERING: Talleyrand will not meet our ambassadors unless we offer him a quite generous bribe.

ABIGAIL: Is this what happens after a revolution?

JOHN: Everything is overturned but the worst of human nature.

ABIGAIL: Oh my Redeemer, what will the newspapers make of this?

PICKERING: They will call it an insult to the prestige of the nation.

ABIGAIL: It is not right. For you our President to have this diet of bile served up with your breakfast every morning. It injures your health.

JOHN: My health is good enough.

ABIGAIL: I am a strong woman and to read these things is agony to me!

JOHN: I could meet with them, Benny Bache—he was a sweet boy, he adored John Quincy—

PICKERING: Washington wouldn't stand for it.

JOHN: Washington.

ABIGAIL: Bache is beneath your notice.

PICKERING: All of them are, Bache, Priestley.

JOHN: Priestley? Doctor Priestley? He has been—he wanted to dedicate his book to me.

PICKERING: Just because a man wants to use your good name to sell his wares, that doesn't make him your friend.

JOHN: Has Priestley written against me?

PICKERING: We suspect it. Anonymous pamphlets traced to Northumberland bear traces of his style.

JOHN: What does he say about me?

PICKERING: Nothing personally. But it seems your administration is a disappointment to him. Insufficiently French.

JOHN: I don't believe it.

ABIGAIL: If Benjamin Franklin's grandson can write against you.

PICKERING: If Thomas Jefferson can support these attacks.

JOHN: Jefferson.

ABIGAIL: You know his heart is in France—

JOHN: France.

ABIGAIL: No matter what atrocities they commit. He is in love with revolutions. He would like to have one at least once a generation.

JOHN: It has been a generation since '76.

ABIGAIL: He was English, then American, now he is a lover of France.

PICKERING: While France is at war with us.

JOHN: Is France is at war with us? Why do they not invade?

PICKERING: We know their spies are everywhere.

ABIGAIL: Everyone says so. But why can't you find them?

PICKERING: We do not have the laws we need.

ABIGAIL: THEN WRITE THEM.

PICKERING: WE HAVE. Do you want them?

(ABIGAIL and PICKERING look at JOHN. He says nothing.)

PICKERING: Temporary measures, for this time of war. Just until the next election. When you win, if you feel them to be of continued use, we will vote to extend them.

ABIGAIL: These laws. Would they silence these traitors?

PICKERING: For a little time. And teach them to have better care for your good name and good nature.

JOHN: I am a strong man. I have withstood criticism all my life.

ABIGAIL: But surely you are entitled to protect yourself. With the weapons at your command.

JOHN: Priestley?

ABIGAIL: Even he.

SERMON

(JOSEPH PRIESTLEY preaches to the ENSEMBLE.)

(JOHN ADAMS is conspicuously in attendance.)

JOSEPH: The first and greatest of the corruptions of Christianity is the idolatrous worship of Jesus Christ, as God equal to the Father. This is a direct violation of the first and greatest of the Ten Commandments, *Thou shalt have no other gods besides me*. Now who was the speaker in this case? Certainly one person, whoever he was, and not two, or more. Granting any other person equal honors with this one great Being must be idolatry.

(An ENSEMBLE MEMBER *exits.)*

JOSEPH: Another doctrine highly injurious to God is that of atonement, that Christ had to die for God to forgive our sins. But scripture says he forgives sins freely, asking only the repentance of the sinner. Christ was sent to redeem us, not by his death, but by his life and his teachings.

(Two ENSEMBLE MEMBERS, *a couple, have agreed to leave together, and do.)*

JOSEPH: The next corruption of Christianity is the doctrine of original sin and predestination. These imply that man does not have the power to do what God requires of him. If so, God is the most unreasonable and unjust of all beings.

*(*JOHN ADAMS *conspicuously exits.)*

JOSEPH: The doctrine of eternal torment is, in all justice, indefensible. The crimes of finite creatures are finite. How can they deserve infinite punishment?

(Another ENSEMBLE MEMBER *exits.)*

JOSEPH: To conclude: of one doctrine I cannot divest myself: Charity. Charity consists in wishing well to all persons, doing them every kindness in our power, thinking as well of them as we can. God looks to the heart, and to the opportunities he gives us to discover the truth. The love of truth is essential to good moral character. In our search for truth we must divest ourselves of every prejudice. It is thus we best fulfill the will of God.

(His sermon ended, JOSEPH *finds he has an audience of one.)*

THOMAS: Thank you. You have given all of us much to think about.

JOSEPH: When I began this series of talks everyone attended.

THOMAS: Many famous faces. Washington, Adams.

JOSEPH: They did not stay.

THOMAS: This administration is easily offended.

JOSEPH: I did not expect to see you here, Mister Jefferson.

THOMAS: In Philadelphia?

JOSEPH: In church.

THOMAS: I do not attend church religiously. I came for the philosophy. There is a natural alliance between religion and science, as there must be between the word and the works of God.

JOSEPH: I am glad to hear you say so. I believe Jesus is underrated as a philosopher. Hold him up to Socrates, he compares quite well.

THOMAS: I was named for the patron saint of doubt. But you make a good case for your man. Jesus and Socrates. We do persecute our philosophers. I am sorry for your persecutions.

JOSEPH: I would not call them persecutions. I tried to create a settlement, but my friends said they felt safer elsewhere. I tried to start a school, but I could find no support. I was offered a professorship of chemistry, but then it fell through. The churches here will not invite me to preach, or not more than once. It is a strange run of bad fortune.

THOMAS: Bad luck? Is that your hypothesis? You are, forgive me, Gunpowder Joe.

JOSEPH: Oh that I had never written that stupid phrase.

THOMAS: The phrases that we write may have a long, long life. They may be a fuse that leads back to our actions. And blow up in our faces. Doctor, you and I are the only true revolutionaries left. They will never forgive us.

JOSEPH: You are of the opposition party.

THOMAS: We have no political parties here. In fact, and this is not universally known, I am the Vice President.

JOSEPH: Of the opposition party?

THOMAS: Of the United States. In the last presidential election I came in second. So President Adams and I, who are age-old friends, are also bitter enemies. We stand for different things, yet we are in the same administration. As mixed and as opposite as the air. Well, there is a windstorm coming. Laws are being written that will make opposition to the government illegal. So philosophers had best be very careful where their thinking leads them. It may lead them into exile. To England, and prison. Or to France, and the guillotine. In a world of enemies, find some allies. Thus endeth my sermon.

*(*THOMAS *exits.* JOSEPH *lifts his eyes in prayer.)*

END OF ACT ONE

ACT TWO

ALIEN AND SEDITION

(TIMOTHY PICKERING *appears, reading out a bill.)*

(BACHE *reads and listens at a distance.)*

PICKERING: "If any person shall write, print, utter or publish, or shall knowingly assist or aid in writing, printing, uttering, or publishing any false scandalous and malicious writing or writings against the government of the United States, or either house of Congress of the United States, or the President of the United States, with intent to defame the government, or to bring them into contempt or disrepute; or to excite against them the hatred of the good people of the United States, or to excite any unlawful opposition or resistance to any law of the United States … "

BACHE: Bit of a run-on sentence.

PICKERING: "…then such person, being convicted before any courts of the United States; shall be punished by a fine not exceeding two thousand dollars, and by imprisonment not exceeding two years." *(He exits.)*

BACHE: I can't help but be flattered. It's so clearly written with me in mind.

(JEFFERSON *appears, grim.)*

THOMAS: Not only you. Did you notice, it is against the law to criticize the President or the Congress, but it is not against the law to criticize the Vice President.

BACHE: Mister Vice President.

THOMAS: I apologize for the lateness of the visit. In order to elude the curiosity of my spies, I had to come by a circuitous route.

BACHE: This law.

THOMAS: This law was passed to defend our freedom. Because we are at war with France.

BACHE: Are we at war?

THOMAS: No one knows. But someone is at war with me.

BACHE: So to preserve our freedom from France, all we're being asked to do is give up our freedom of thought, and speech, and peaceful assembly, and so on. I feel freer already.

*(*THOMAS *removes a sheaf of official-looking papers from his pocket and hands them to* BACHE.*)*

BACHE: What are these?

THOMAS: How is your French?

BACHE: *Comme ci, comme ça. J'ai habité à Paris avec mon grand-père.*

THOMAS: While your grandfather was in Paris, yes, you were there.

BACHE: I went to school with the Adamses son, John Quincy. We all go back so far together.

THOMAS: This law is an experiment on the American mind to see how much we will take. Next we shall see an act of Congress, establishing the Senate for life, appointing Adams President for life, and next they will transfer the succession to his heirs, and we shall be a monarchy again. John Quincy Adams could be your king.

BACHE: That's a good line.

THOMAS: Use it. But do not use my name.

(THOMAS and BACHE exit.)

(COBBETT reads from a newspaper.)

COBBETT: "The infidel Jefferson is one step from the Presidency. If he should rise, the seal of death is set on our holy religion. Do you trust a spendthrift, a libertine, an Atheist to govern you and your children; to be entrusted with the destiny of the nation? At this moment, the only question to be asked by every American, is 'Shall I continue in allegiance to God and a religious president; or declare for Jefferson—and NO GOD!!!'"

(JOSEPH and COOPER, with manuscript pages.)

JOSEPH: But if this writing is traced back to us.

COOPER: We do not even need to mention Adams by name.

JOSEPH: I think they'll know who we're writing about. The new law gives the President the power to deport any alien he deems a danger, with no trial, no appeal. I would not survive another sea voyage.

COOPER: I have never seen you frightened.

JOSEPH: I have never been this old before. But you are right. It is not important.

COOPER: What's important are the questions you are asking: an administration wants to spend money to create a standing army. We are not at war. Why do we need to pay taxes, and go into debt, to buy a permanent army?

JOSEPH: The question is, who is it to be used against?

COOPER: Already been used against. Some farmers in Western Pennsylvania.

JOSEPH: Look at France.

COOPER: Yes! They all think we are in love with France, so let us use France as an example of why this is a bad idea. Their army killed their own citizens. Because they asked for bread.

JOSEPH: No one cares what I think about American politics.

COOPER: Of course they do. Your ideas are important.

JOSEPH: If the ideas are important, and well proven, it doesn't matter who writes them.

COOPER: Then I will write them.

JOSEPH: The government knows you. They will say you are just angry because they wouldn't give you a job.

COOPER: I'll write anonymously.

JOSEPH: If you publish them here, they will know who wrote it. The only ones in Northumberland who write and publish are you and I.

COOPER: I may be able to take it to another part of the country, find another publisher.

JOSEPH: If you can find a publisher willing to print them. They are being watched.

COOPER: I'll print it here and distribute it somewhere else.

JOSEPH: Can you grieve for a place you barely know?

COOPER: What do you always say? It'll be fine.

JOSEPH: It will be a test. To see how much dissent this government can bear. It will be an experiment.

(JOSEPH *and* COOPER *exit.)*

(BACHE *and* COBBETT, *with their newspapers.)*

COBBETT: These United States have become the resting place of ninety-nine hundredths of the factious villains which Great Britain has vomited from its shores. They are all schooled in sedition, adept at their trade, and they bear as great a hatred to this government as they did to their own!

(BACHE *is silent.* COBBETT *exits.* PICKERING *enters.)*

PICKERING: Good morning, Mister Bache. I have time for just a few questions.

BACHE: Thank you, Mister Pickering. To start with, may I know why I have been arrested?

PICKERING: I have time to *ask* you just a few questions.

BACHE: Right. Understood. Fire away.

PICKERING: You published, in your newspaper, communications from France.

BACHE: Old friends of my grandfather.

PICKERING: Copies of secret communications between France and your government. You published state secrets. To turn the people against their government.

BACHE: Why would those communications turn the people against their government? Are you afraid for the people to know you're negotiating with terrorists? The Sedition Act says you can't convict me for printing what's true.

PICKERING: We can convict you for being in contact with our enemies.

BACHE: They are not our enemies. You haven't declared war. And you're in contact with them too.

PICKERING: Is Jefferson in contact with the French?

BACHE: He's part of your administration and your administration is in contact with France.

PICKERING: Is Jefferson receiving private letters from France?

BACHE: Are you hoping to arrest the Vice President for sedition?

PICKERING: Answer the question.

BACHE: I have no idea. You open his mail, why ask me?

PICKERING: Does he say we open his mail?

BACHE: No.

PICKERING: Why do you say we do?

BACHE: I just assumed, since you open mine and you think we're a conspiracy.

PICKERING: You accuse your government of acting underhandedly. You publish outrageous falsehoods about the government.

BACHE: Not falsehoods. Innuendo and satire. Peter Porcupine publishes outrageous falsehoods—

PICKERING: Not about the government.

BACHE: Is he under arrest? Because I'm just trying to compete in a tough marketplace.

PICKERING: He only mocks private citizens.

BACHE: Private citizens who criticize the government.

PICKERING: They are free to sue him for libel. If he is printing lies, he is liable.

BACHE: So writing anything in opposition to the Sedition Act is a violation of the Sedition Act.

PICKERING: Only if what you say is untrue.

BACHE: If I write that the Sedition Act is unconstitutional, your judge will find the Sedition Act is not unconstitutional and I have violated the Sedition Act. If I write that the Sedition Act is an unwise policy, I am questioning the wisdom of our leaders and I have violated the Sedition Act. When I tried to publish the Congressional debates about the Sedition Act, I was arrested for printing statements criticizing the Sedition Act—I was quoting Congressmen, who are our leaders! If I write that the Sedition Act forbids me to write that someone has criticized the Sedition Act, I have violated the Sedition Act. That's quite an act, that Sedition Act. Good God, sir! Is it a crime to doubt the capacity of a President? Have we advanced so far on the road to despotism in this country that we dare not say our President is mistaken?

PICKERING: Mister Bache, you have just violated the Sedition Act.

BACHE: The Sedition Act can go violate itself! I appreciate your sitting down for this interview, Mister Pickering, I have just two more questions.

PICKERING: Your bail will be set this afternoon.

BACHE: Is there a disagreement within the administration about going to war with France? Some elements seem eager for war, others less so. The dispatches I published make it clear that given the right conditions, we and France could negotiate a peace. Napoleon Bonaparte has his hands full conquering Europe. He doesn't want a war. The President doesn't want a war. But we have an army and a navy now. Do they want a war? Is that what you don't want the people to know? Who is governing us? It is a philosophical question.

PICKERING: Good day, Mister Bache.

THE ADMINISTRATION

(The President, and Vice President, and the Secretary of State. JOHN, THOMAS, *and* PICKERING. *Polite. Daggers drawn.)*

THOMAS: The papers have been much occupied lately in placing us in opposition to each other. I trust that neither of us feels it personally?

JOHN: Certainly not. Rivalries have been irritated to madness.

THOMAS: I agree.

JOHN: But I do not take revenge. I don't remember that I was ever vindictive in my life. I am not very angry now.

THOMAS: I learn little of what is passing: pamphlets I see never; papers but a few.

JOHN: The fewer the happier.

THOMAS: You have arrested Benny Bache.

PICKERING: We are very interested in knowing who has supported Bache in his libels and treasons. Who his subscribers are.

THOMAS: You have arrested Bache for what he has written in the *Aurora*.

JOHN: This is not journalism. This is terrorism.

PICKERING: Exactly.

THOMAS: So you have read the *Aurora*.

PICKERING: Of course.

THOMAS: So you subscribe to the *Aurora* yourself. So do I. Bache is the grandson and namesake of our old friend Franklin.

PICKERING: We do not encourage our friends to support him.

THOMAS: I shouldn't think so.

PICKERING: But you do.

THOMAS: I would hardly encourage the support of a journal so critical of an administration of which I am a part. Have you heard or read that I have?

PICKERING: You have not committed yourself to print on the matter.

JOHN: We are at war.

THOMAS: If we were at war, there would have been a declaration by the Senate. I recall no vote for such a measure.

JOHN: French spies swarm in our cities and in the country.

THOMAS: Have you found any?

JOHN: These laws were designed to check them!

THOMAS: Then the laws are working very well.

JOHN: Was there ever a government, which had not authority to defend itself against spies in its own bosom? Spies of an enemy at war?

THOMAS: Your Excellency. I devoutly wish you are able to shun this war. If you are, the glory will be all your own; the happiness will be to us all.

JOHN: The French are committing acts of war. They want to bring their terror to our shores.

THOMAS: They have attacked our shipping.

JOHN: Yes! Exactly!

THOMAS: There's your problem: shipping. If all the money we spent protecting merchant ships were put to digging canals and building bridges, our commerce would be stronger and our enemies weaker.

JOHN: According to whom?

THOMAS: Doctor Priestley. His "Maxims of Political Arithmetic," have you read it? Published anonymously but everyone knows it is Priestley's work.

JOHN: Why published anonymously?

THOMAS: When a writer can be imprisoned for criticizing the government—your government—the writer known as Anonymous becomes most prolific.

JOHN: I have counted Priestley as a friend. He is a guest in this country.

THOMAS: That is why I am telling you. As a friend. In trying to suppress your enemies, you are making more enemies. You may be making enemies of your friends.

(Drumming and shouts in the distance)

THE BLACK COCKADE

*(*COBBETT *reads from Porcupine's Gazette.)*

*(*BACHE *reads from his notes.)*

COBBETT: Young Men of Philadelphia!

BACHE: They are called the Volunteer Corps.

COBBETT: Your country calls for your assistance—the hour of danger is arrived...

BACHE: Thousands of young men, hungry for a fight.

COBBETT: The mask is taken from the face of our false, perfidious friends, both at home and abroad ... Shall the youthful arm of America be unnerved in the hour of danger ...? No!

BACHE: They all wear black ribbon badges—cockades.

COBBETT: Proudly don the black cockade!

BACHE: Not red, white, and blue, those are the colors of France.

COBBETT: Rise up, gird on the armor of defense! Perish the traitors!

BACHE: The fat little President wears a ridiculous uniform and they pass in review and nobody laughs because it is against the law to laugh at John Adams.

*(*JOHN ADAMS, *wearing dress uniform and sword, harangues.)*

JOHN: To arms, then, my young friends—to arms! For safety! The dangers which we now see and feel, cannot be averted by truth, reason, or justice. If there are any who plead the cause of France and attempt to paralyze the efforts of your government, I agree with you they are our greatest enemies. Remember: the worst enemy we have, is slander! It is the worst enemy to virtue and the best friend to vice; it strives to destroy all distinction between right and wrong; it leads to division, sedition, and civil war. I need say no more. Perish the traitors!

BACHE: They broke the windows in my print shop. I fought free and ran for my life. THIS IS HAPPENING HERE.

FEVER DREAM

(Drumming and shouts continue, closer)

*(*JOSEPH, *ill, attended by* COOPER, BACHE, *and* MADISON.*)*

*(*COOPER *is examining* JOSEPH.*)*

COOPER: It is a fever.

BACHE: Not the yellow fever. I've seen that.

COOPER: Pleurisy, most likely.

*(*JOSEPH *tries to stand up and fails.)*

JOSEPH: What do I hear?

BACHE: Just some young men in high spirits.

COOPER: You are welcome to stay the night, Mister Bache.

BACHE: Thank you. I have a newspaper to print.

COOPER: You are out on bail pending trial.

BACHE: Yes.

COOPER: For printing your newspaper.

BACHE: Yes. Arrested Editor Puts Out Paper. Either no one will buy it or everyone will.

COOPER: Congratulations. I am usually the most foolhardy man in any room I am in.

JOSEPH: What is happening?

BACHE: There are armed men roaming the streets. But they are all dressed the same so we are supposed to obey them.

JOSEPH: The mob is coming. Where is Mary? She must have a plan. Cooper?

COOPER: I'm here.

JOSEPH: Who else is here? We must make our escape. They will break the apparatus. Burn the papers.

COOPER: No one will break your apparatus. We are in Philadelphia. No one can burn your papers.

BACHE: They have burnt my papers.

COOPER: Bache, you're not helping.

BACHE: So everyone tells me.

JOSEPH: Who is here? Cooper? And Doctor Franklin? It is very good to see you. Very good.

BACHE: No, Doctor Priestley, I—

JOSEPH: You have not aged a day. Why are you in Birmingham?

BACHE: We are not in Birmingham, sir. *(To* COOPER*)* Is there treatment that would calm him? Is there a doctor close by?

COOPER: I have done a little doctoring. He is calm, he is always calm, he has no fear of death, he sees it as a reunion.

JOSEPH: Has the mob followed me to London, then?

BACHE: He is in fear of something.

JOSEPH: We are in danger. We must make our way to America.

COOPER: We are in America!

BACHE: And we are in Philadelphia.

JOSEPH: Doctor Franklin. My sight is dim, but I would know your glasses anywhere.

BACHE: Doctor Priestley. That is why I wear them. Whatever I do I always hope people wonder if in some way Benjamin Franklin has his eyes on them.

(Glass breaks somewhere.)

JOSEPH: What is happening?

BACHE: Someone is performing an experiment with fire.

COOPER: Doctor Priestley? May we try an experiment now?

JOSEPH: Of course. What sort?

COOPER: On the fluids of the body.

BACHE: Cooper, are you sure you know what you're doing?

COOPER: Please. Doctor Priestley, it is for the advancement of learning.

*(*JOSEPH *holds out his arm.)*

*(*COOPER *sets about to bleed* JOSEPH. *He holds out a bowl to* MADISON, *who takes it and holds it under* JOSEPH*'s arm while* COOPER *prepares to make a small incision.)*

MADISON: *(To us)* Now, everybody knows that for a fevered mind, you take sheep weed leaves, bay leaf, and sarsaparilla root, cut the bark up fine and make a tea, you drink some and the patient drinks some. My mother taught me that. Now, my mother also carried a picture of Saint Mary Magdalene to bring her luck in love. So the main thing I learned from my mother is not to believe everything you hear from your mother. You have to try things out yourself.

BACHE: Do you know, Doctor Priestley, there is a story about…me. They tell it in France.

JOSEPH: Oh, Doctor Franklin, remember I am a clergyman.

BACHE: Not that kind of story. When I was there during the War of Independence, the French people would ask me how the war was going. My French was not of the best, and neither was the news of the war. But I would always say, "*Ça ira, ça ira*" It'll be fine, it'll be fine. Years later, when they had their revolution, they made it into a marching song.

JOSEPH: It'll be fine, it'll be fine. Not a bad philosophy.

BACHE: I believe I learned it from you.

JOSEPH: You have always been a kind friend. Do you know the song?

BACHE: I do. *(Singing)*
Ah! Ça ira, ça ira…
(Speaking) Some of the words are very rude. About stringing up the aristocrats and shoving shovels up their … and so on.

JOSEPH: Sing it in French, then I can't be offended.

BACHE: *(Singing)*
Ah! ça ira, ça ira, ça ira
les aristocrates à la lantern…
Ah! ça ira, ça ira, ça ira
les aristocrates on les pendra…

(One by one, the others join. JOSEPH *dozes, and they continue to sing softly.* COOPER *translates as they sing. For a final chorus, the song grows as the* ENSEMBLE *joins, and the march carries* COOPER *out of the scene.)*

BACHE, COOPER, MADISON & ENSEMBLE: *(Singing)*
Ah! ça ira, ça ira, ça ira
les aristocrates à la lantern…
Ah! ça ira, ça ira, ça ira
les aristocrates on les pendra…

(Ah! It'll be fine, It'll be fine, It'll be fine
The aristocrats go to the wall
Ah! It'll be fine, It'll be fine, It'll be fine
The aristocrats, we'll hang 'em all)

COOPER'S LIBEL

(A gavel sounds several times.)

*(*COOPER *speaks in public.)*

(A rhythmic noise rises behind him.)

COOPER: Your Honor.
I supported Mister Adams when he was elected President. But at that time he had just entered into office; he was hardly in the infancy of political mistake: even those who doubted his mental capacity thought well of his intentions. He had not yet abolished the right to trial by jury in the alien law, or entrenched his public character behind the legal barriers of the sedition law. Nor were we yet saddled with the expense of a permanent navy, or threatened with the

existence of a standing army. He had not yet uttered threats against other nations so violent that they may provoke a war! We used to have to say the king of England could do no wrong, but I did not know till now that we must say the same of the President of the United States.

(The noise overwhelms him.)

(BACHE, *ill and troubled, holds his newspaper.)*

BACHE: In a trial, the judge is supposed to ensure that the trial will be fair. During Mister Cooper's trial, the judge instructed the grand jury, quote: "If a man attempts to destroy the confidence of the people in their officers, he attacks the foundation of the government." End quote. They found him guilty. The judge, Associate Justice of the Supreme Court Samuel Chase, was one of the signers of the Declaration of Independence. Pray for us.

INTERVIEW

(JOSEPH, *deeply subdued, and* PICKERING)

PICKERING: You are completely recovered?

JOSEPH: Much improved. Thank you.

PICKERING: What are your plans? Will you preach again?

JOSEPH: I have no plans to speak at present.

PICKERING: Or publish?

JOSEPH: I hope to complete my notes on scripture. In the time I have left to me.

PICKERING: And politics? Your voice at this critical time…

JOSEPH: I am a guest in this country. I cannot take sides among my hosts. I'm sorry, you told me how you came to be in the neighborhood, but I...

PICKERING: We are a small congregation, in Philadelphia, concerned for your well-being. They asked me to journey to Northumberland to see how you are.

JOSEPH: That is most kind. I miss Philadelphia. Greet them for me, please.

PICKERING: So, are you doing anything else?

JOSEPH: Not as much as I once could. I'm an old man.

PICKERING: Forgive me. I should take my leave.

JOSEPH: No. Stay a while. Please. I get so little company now. It is a tonic.

PICKERING: I find it hard to believe you have no large plan.

JOSEPH: Mister Jefferson approached me about helping him found a university in Virginia, but...

PICKERING: You are in contact with Mister Jefferson.

JOSEPH: No. We have met. He was gracious.

PICKERING: No one can believe you do not have some great project in mind.

JOSEPH: Only thoughts and ideas for experiments. No projects. I am done.

PICKERING: Jefferson is not done with revolution. He and his friends are forming an opposition. Some say a conspiracy. Some say a rebellion.

JOSEPH: Some say.

PICKERING: Opposition is one thing. Treason is another. Or maybe they're the same thing.

JOSEPH: My friend Bache has been arrested. My friend Cooper is in prison. I have never heard them utter a word disloyal to this country.

PICKERING: Would you say they have been unjustly arrested? You think President Adams made a mistake?

JOSEPH: No. No. I would not say so.

PICKERING: I would not dare to say so if I were you.

JOSEPH: I do not.

PICKERING: Good. For your own sake. Saying a thing like that, if someone found out, he could get arrested. Or worse. Hadn't you heard? Benjamin Franklin Bache is dead.

JOSEPH: No. No I had not heard. God rest his soul. What happened to him?

PICKERING: He was required to remain in Philadelphia, awaiting his trial. Yellow fever was bad this summer in Philadelphia.

JOSEPH: Who are you?

PICKERING: Doesn't matter. I could be anybody. That's the point. I'm here as a favor to you.

JOSEPH: A favor from whom?

PICKERING: You know what? You ask too many questions. Gunpowder Joe. *(He exits.)*

JOSEPH: There is no such thing as too many questions.

MOMENT OF TRUTH

(JOHN, *still in his uniform,* ABIGAIL, PICKERING)

ABIGAIL: Most of the opposition newspapers are closed. A good number of traitors arrested. Cooper is convicted. Bache is dead. One more decision must be made, I think.

JOHN: Doctor Priestley writes nothing, says nothing worth our notice. He is reduced to prophesizing to the rocks and trees and the Susquehanna River.

ABIGAIL: And the citizens of Northumberland.

JOHN: He barely has a pulpit.

PICKERING: I once thought him a persecuted Christian, but I am now satisfied that ambition influences him. No government would ever make him contented, unless he were placed at its head.

ABIGAIL: Does he think philosophers are above the law?

JOHN: Not even Socrates was above the law. Nor our Savior. He admires both. He knows what can happen. He will not speak in his own name and if he does no one will listen.

PICKERING: Let them listen. Make them see. Prosecute him.

JOHN: He told me he longs to live quietly.

ABIGAIL: You probably told him something like the same thing. And here you are.

JOHN: All he wants is a comfortable old age.

ABIGAIL: Let him find it in France. If he can.

JOHN: If he wants a quiet life, why did he write against me? He has to know, he has to know it is against the law.

ABIGAIL: Some people say and do things to quiet their own minds. With no regard for the clamor the world may make as a result.

JOHN: I do not want to be seen as the President who exiled the great mind of the age.

ABIGAIL: Is he the great mind of the age, anymore? Or is he a deranged old man throwing rocks at your windows? Madness can descend upon the finest minds. We know this.

JOHN: When I saw him last, he and I talked about apocalypse. Signs of the millennium. The horns of the beast. He is not political in the same way you and I are.

ABIGAIL: He can be used for political means.

JOHN: Our best political means may be to do nothing.

ABIGAIL: Not to go to war, not to punish your enemies—why is your first choice of action always to do nothing!

JOHN: What should I do, spend my days passing judgments and plotting revenges?

ABIGAIL: When necessary, yes! Why not?

JOHN: Do you not find it exhausting?

ABIGAIL: Utterly!

JOHN: When I sit with Priestley, a peace descends. His voice. He has a murmuring chuckle, like a brook. I could not think of the apocalypse, but only of the psalm. To lie down in green pastures. To restore my soul.

ABIGAIL: You want to rest.

JOHN: At long last?

ABIGAIL: It will be President Jefferson then. Whose green pastures are tended by his slaves. And are mortgaged to the hilt.

JOHN: All right. Yes. All right.

PICKERING: Good. And truly, the indecency of it. Strangers, aliens, meddling with our government. Men like him are the reason these laws were passed. If we do not apply the law, we fail in our duty.

JOHN: You tell me my duty, Mister Pickering! My duty! To me!

PICKERING: I remind you.

ABIGAIL: You will do what you think best.

JOHN: I do not think it wise to execute the Alien Law. Not against poor Priestley. Not at present. He is as weak as water, unstable as the wind. His influence is not an atom in the world. If he dare to make the next move, it will come to nothing. Let him try.

CHESS

*(*MADISON *is holding a bowl and stirring its contents. He is counting strokes and studying the results for consistency from time to time.)*

JOSEPH: *(Off)* Is anyone in the house?

*(*MADISON, *trying to concentrate, does not answer.)*

JOSEPH: *(Off)* Anyone?

*(*MADISON *continues to stir.)*

*(*JOSEPH *enters, anxious, holds a sheaf of papers.)*

JOSEPH: Madison. Good. I wonder if you would run an errand for me. It is just into town and back.

*(*MADISON *stops stirring and watches him.)*

JOSEPH: I will write you a pass in case you are stopped and questioned. Could you do that?

MADISON: Yes, sir.

JOSEPH: Good, excellent.

*(*JOSEPH, *relieved, takes pen and ink and writes.* MADISON *covers his bowl and puts it aside with a small moment of regret.)*

MADISON: What is the errand?

JOSEPH: I have some pages here that I need to go to Mister Cooper's printing shop right away. Do you know where that is?

MADISON: Yes, sir.

JOSEPH: Tell the printer I am a friend of Mister Cooper and they are from me. It would be better if I do not deliver them myself. I believe my mail and messages are being opened. You will attract less attention than I.

MADISON: Yes, sir.

JOSEPH: If you could hide the pages somewhere about your person. Give them to no one but the printer himself.

MADISON: If I am stopped and asked where I am going, what shall I say?

JOSEPH: I don't want you to have to lie.

MADISON: No, sir. *(Beat)* Is there another errand I could be running? Then if anyone asks, I can say I am doing that. And not mention the printer.

JOSEPH: Aye. Good. But what?

MADISON: Do you need anything for in your laboratory? Bottles or jars or rags?

JOSEPH: Yes. Scientific apparatus. The dry goods store. Good. Here is money.

*(*JOSEPH *fishes coins from his purse and hands them to* MADISON. *He counts them and holds them out to show him.)*

MADISON: That is one dollar.

JOSEPH: Aye, fine.

MADISON: Could you write on the pass that you have given me one dollar for dry goods.

JOSEPH: Ah. Aye. *(He does so, waves the paper to dry it, and hands it to* MADISON.*)* As soon as you are done, come back and let me know that you and the pages are safe.

MADISON: Yes, sir. *(He turns to go.)*

JOSEPH: That is a clever strategy, about the errands. A double attack by misdirection. Doing one thing while you seem to do another. Do you play chess?

MADISON: It's an old trick, sir. But it still works. *(As he goes, to us)* Every damn day.

THE NEWS FROM FRANCE

*(*JOHN *and* PICKERING*)*

JOHN: Mister Pickering! Glorious news! A message from my new envoy to France.

PICKERING: What envoy to France?

JOHN: The envoy I sent to France. Did I not tell you?

PICKERING: I know of no envoy, I know of no message.

JOHN: It is a personal message. The point of playing chess by mail is that you can play multiple games at a time.

PICKERING: And the message?

JOHN: The French want peace! There will be no war! The emergency is over! Halleluiah!

PICKERING: Hell and damnation!

JOHN: I always said the French wanted peace. Napoleon wants no part of us.

PICKERING: You…

JOHN: I was never a soldier, like Washington, nor a philosopher like Jefferson. But I was a lawyer. And not a bad one. Negotiation, Mister Pickering.

PICKERING: Our party is only popular as long as we are at war.

JOHN: We never were actually at war.

PICKERING: Correct! On that basis we could have stayed in a state of halfway war forever. Our party could have stayed in power forever.

JOHN: I am the head of no party.

PICKERING: No, sir, you are not.

JOHN: So who is? You?

PICKERING: Among others. Do you think you elected yourself? Why did you think I am here? Why did you stop listening to me?

JOHN: I have followed the dictates of my conscience.

PICKERING: You…you will be the death of us. It will be all Jefferson, all the South, all slavery, for a generation.

JOHN: Is that our only choice? Between slavery and perpetual war?

PICKERING: Of course that is our only choice! How could you be the President of the United States and not have grasped that?

JOHN: Mister Pickering, I must ask for your resignation.

PICKERING: I refuse to give it to you.

JOHN: Then you are dismissed from your position.

PICKERING: And so are you, soon enough. I leave you to your enemies. You pompous ass.

JOHN: My enemies may have me. They are in the main my oldest friends.

LETTERS TO NORTHUMBERLAND

(JOSEPH PRIESTLEY *stands alone.)*

JOSEPH: My friends and neighbors,
It is now in the power of the President to order me out of the country. I offer therefore a full confession of all my political crimes and misdemeanors.

(As JOSEPH PRIESTLEY *speaks,* ENSEMBLE *members enter, reading his words from pamphlets and gazettes. Gradually they join their voices to his. Eventually the entire* ENSEMBLE *[save* BACHE*] is present, holding their copies of* PRIESTLEY*'s words, sharing them, contemplating them, sometimes shouting them in unison.)*

SALLY: In our shock at the Reign of Terror in France, it has become fashionable to exclaim against all revolutions.

THOMAS: But the French Revolution and the American Revolution both arose from the same principles.

PICKERING: The immediate stimulus was oppression.

COOPER: I rejoice in both revolutions alike.

JOSEPH: Old men are slow to change. Give me time.

JOHN: According to your constitution, all persons entrusted with public affairs are but your servants, and accountable to you for their conduct in office.

COOPER: May not a person who thinks them to be mistaken, or dishonest, or a danger to the people, point it out? Nay, is this not the duty of every honest man?

COBBETT: Laws restraining the freedom of speech and of the press are the resort of arbitrary governments. I was astonished to find them introduced here.

PICKERING: Governors try in vain to silence their adversaries.

COOPER: But the less men have the liberty to speak, the more they will think; and they will think that what they are forbidden to examine will not bear examination.

JOSEPH: And so I shall say it: The Alien and Sedition Acts are evidently unconstitutional.

JOHN: Congress have made laws expressly forbidden by the constitution.

COBBETT: Laws concerning aliens like me.

COOPER: Laws calculated to throw difficulties in the way of our becoming citizens.

COBBETT: Aliens in general quietly mind our business, not giving ourselves, or you, any trouble.

COOPER: When a man is kept by force in the status of an alien, he will not think better of his country. If he be hostile, that status will make him no less able to do mischief.

JOSEPH: The Federalists seem to think that democracy is the greatest of all crimes.

THOMAS: That democracy means anarchy and confusion, government by mobs, and an equalization of all property.

JOHN: If you can be convinced of that, you might be made to fear that an army of French cannibals may cross the Atlantic in a fleet of balloons, land on the blue mountains, and eat your children for breakfast.

THOMAS: Democracy means nothing more than the government of the people.

SALLY: Equality means the equality of rights, of power to acquire property and to keep it;

THOMAS & COOPER: The equality that actually exists in this country.

JOSEPH: My Friends and Neighbors,

THOMAS, COOPER, & JOHN: I am, with my wishes and prayers for your welfare,

JOSEPH: Yours sincerely,

FULL ENSEMBLE: Joseph Priestley!

DEPARTURES

(The ENSEMBLE *heads in all directions, packing and parting.)*

*(*COOPER *and* JOSEPH*)*

COOPER: And I say President Jefferson owes his election to you.

JOSEPH: You are too generous.

COOPER: Jefferson needed Pennsylvania, and Pennsylvania listened to you. I said you would do great things. And now you are safe at last.

JOSEPH: Time will tell. But must you depart?

COOPER: The opportunity is to the South. A small plantation.

JOSEPH: You will own slaves?

COOPER: That kind of business is impractical without the use of slaves. I have to get free of my debts.

JOSEPH: It's a strange sort of freedom that insists on the right to enslave someone else.

COOPER: When an American speaks of freedom, that is exactly what he means. I mean to be an American.

*(*JOHN *and* ABIGAIL*)*

(He is reading one book, holding another. She is carrying things.)

ABIGAIL: The packing is nearly done. How did we accumulate so many books during our stay here?

JOHN: And read so few.

ABIGAIL: Now there will be more time for reading.

JOHN: And fewer subjects to have to master.

ABIGAIL: Much to be done with the farm.

JOHN: Scarcely any thing that has happened to me, in my curious life, has made a deeper impression upon me, than that a madcap like Thomas Cooper could have made Joseph Priestley my enemy.

ABIGAIL: You are my dearest friend. And I say the sweetest words there be: Let's you and I go home.

(PICKERING *watches them go.)*

PICKERING: We had all waited for John Adams to do that one great deed for which he would be remembered. It would surprise him to hear me say this. But when the newspapers are dust and so are we, and the histories are written, do you know what in my expert opinion will be seen as the President's most enduring and influential achievement? His marriage.

(COBBETT *brandishes his gazette.)*

COBBETT: Special! And Final! Edition of *Porcupine's Gazette*! Gross miscarriage of justice committed by the corrupt and powerful enemies of Peter Porcupine and honest men everywhere. A lawsuit for libel! Jury awards damages of Five Thousand Dollars! Which is more than all the damages for all the libel suits in all the history of Philadelphia to date! I am the greatest libeler ever! But. Financial ruin for America's most popular journalist! Poor Peter Porcupine's quills are pulled out. Time to return to my native soil. O to be in England! O, O, O.

(THOMAS and SALLY. She holds a baby and is pregnant again.)

THOMAS: I should be off in the morning. To the new capital. Much to do.

SALLY: Before you go. About our children. Are we agreed?

THOMAS: I have said.

SALLY: You did not exactly say. And that is very like you.

THOMAS: The country has changed, since we spoke of this. It is more fearful.

SALLY: You are the president of it now.

THOMAS: There is a law, here in Virginia, that children like this child, who have one great-grandparent from Africa, and all the rest white, that child is white.

SALLY: But could they change the law?

THOMAS: They could. But even so, with my permission, he could be free.

SALLY: But if he were to just up and disappear one day, and go to Philadelphia, go to the West, he could be…

THOMAS: He could be whatever he wants.

SALLY: Whatever he wants. But not with me. I came home from France to be in the land of my family. He may need to go far. He would be gone and I…

THOMAS: I will return in the summer.

SALLY: I'll be here.

(THOMAS exits.)

SALLY: I'll be here.

THE MOUSE AND THE MINT

*(*JOSEPH *stands behind a table that holds three bell jars.)*

(The ENSEMBLE *watches.)*

(He speaks to us.)

JOSEPH: Ladies and gentlemen,
This may be my most extraordinary discovery yet
And I confess I have only an inkling how it works.
I do not think I will learn the answer in the time I have left.
I hope that some of you will take up the experiment, after I am gone.
So. We have here three different places.
Sealed shut against the outside air.
In one jar, I have placed a plant. I use a sprig of mint.
If you keep it sealed up like this long enough, even with ample soil and sun and water,
It shrivels and dies.
In this jar, I have placed a mouse. Even with food and water, sealed up in this way, it quickly becomes distressed and, if we do not release it, it too will die.
We have known this for a long time, about the mouse.
A candle behaves the same.
And so do we.
I believe that the mouse, and we ourselves, breathe in one kind of air, but breathe out another. Whatever it is that we need from the air, the reason that we breathe, we take it in, and we give out something else.
But what about the plant? Why does it behave the same?
Is the plant breathing?
So, because I like to try a lot of things, I tried this.
And here is the most extraordinary thing. The third place.
In this jar there is a mint and a mouse. Sealed in together. I have had these here for quite a long time.

And look here.
They live.
I do not understand this yet.
But I have a hypothesis.
The mouse breathes out something the plant needs.
The plant breathes out something the mouse needs.
Each breathes the same air, but each needs a different part of it to live. A part which the other supplies.
Now. Step back. Is this like the world?
What I have learned from the air is this:
Though something be invisible, yet it has parts of its own.
Though it cannot be seen, and is difficult to know, it has power and can do work and make change.
But I think some of you know this.
I pray that you continue the experiment.
It'll be fine. Thank you, and good day.

END OF PLAY

www.ingramcontent.com/pod-product-compliance
Lightning Source LLC
Chambersburg PA
CBHW052213090426
42741CB00010B/2521